# THE COURSE OF CHOCOLATE

By Harriet Brundle

**BookLife PUBLISHING**

©2022
BookLife Publishing Ltd.
King's Lynn
Norfolk, PE30 4LS

**ISBN:** 978-1-83927-840-2

**Written by:**
Harriet Brundle

**Edited by:**
Emilie Dufresne

**Designed by:**
Danielle Rippengill

All rights reserved.
Printed in Poland.

A catalogue record for this book is available from the British Library.

All facts, statistics, web addresses and URLs in this book were verified as valid and accurate at time of writing. No responsibility for any changes to external websites or references can be accepted by either the author or publisher.

Words that look like **this** can be found in the glossary on page 24.

# Photo Credits

All images are courtesy of Shutterstock.com, unless otherwise specified. With thanks to Getty Images, Thinkstock Photo and iStockphoto. Cover images – kondratya, DKDesignz, surabhi25, Cute little things, Valentyn Volkov, wasapohn. Recurring images – kondratya, DKDesignz, urabhi25, Cute little things, Valentyn Volkov, Walnut Bird, Mark Olivier, wasapohn, NotionPic. 6 – Hans Geel. 7 – nnattalli. 8 – Kaiskynet Studio. 9 – noBorders – Brayden Howie. 10 – mavo. 11 – Narong Khueankaew. 12 – Svetlana Lukienko. 13 – photowind. 14 – fjmolina. 15 – grafvision. 16 – wavebreakmedia. 17 – industryviews. 18 – Jozef Sowa. 18&19 – Africa Studio. 19 – Aleksandrova Karina, Pixel-Shot. 20 – Africa Studio, EQRoy, jabiru, Pavlo Lys, Sergey Lapin. 21 – LightField Studios, Motortion Films, Natasha Breen, New Africa.

# CONTENTS

| | |
|---|---|
| Page 4 | Hop on The Chocolate Box |
| Page 6 | The Course of Chocolate |
| Page 8 | Inside the Pod |
| Page 10 | At the Factory |
| Page 12 | Grind It Up |
| Page 14 | In Production |
| Page 18 | Sweet Chocolate |
| Page 20 | All the Flavours |
| Page 22 | Chocolate Time! |
| Page 24 | Glossary and Index |

# HOP ON THE CHOCOLATE BOX

Hello! My name is Kwame and this is my van, The Chocolate Box. I make lots of tasty chocolate bars. Is there something you would like?

**MENU**

Milk chocolate

Dark chocolate

White chocolate

Chocolate caramel

# THE COURSE OF CHOCOLATE

The start of our journey to find more chocolate begins right here in The Chocolate Box. We are going to travel to Ghana, in West Africa, to find out where chocolate comes from.

Cocoa beans

Chocolate is made from cocoa beans.

Cocoa pods growing on a cacao tree

Cacao trees grow pods, which have cocoa beans inside. Once they are <u>ripe</u>, the pods are usually <u>harvested</u> by hand. The workers use a sharp knife to cut the pods from the trees.

# INSIDE THE POD

After they have been harvested, the pods are split open and the cocoa beans and white <u>pulp</u> inside are taken out. The beans and pulp are then left to <u>ferment</u>.

Beans and pulp ready to ferment

Once fermented, the beans are dried. This might be done by machine or, where possible, the beans are laid out in the hot sun to dry for several days.

# AT THE FACTORY

When the beans have been dried, they go to the factory. There, the beans are cleaned and roasted. Roasting brings out the delicious chocolate flavour.

After roasting, the beans' outer shells are taken away. After this, just the cocoa nibs are left.

Cocoa nibs

Removing the outer shell is called winnowing.

# GRIND IT UP

Next, the nibs are ground up. The **friction** and heat made while the nibs are being ground turns them into a very thick, dark brown **liquid**.

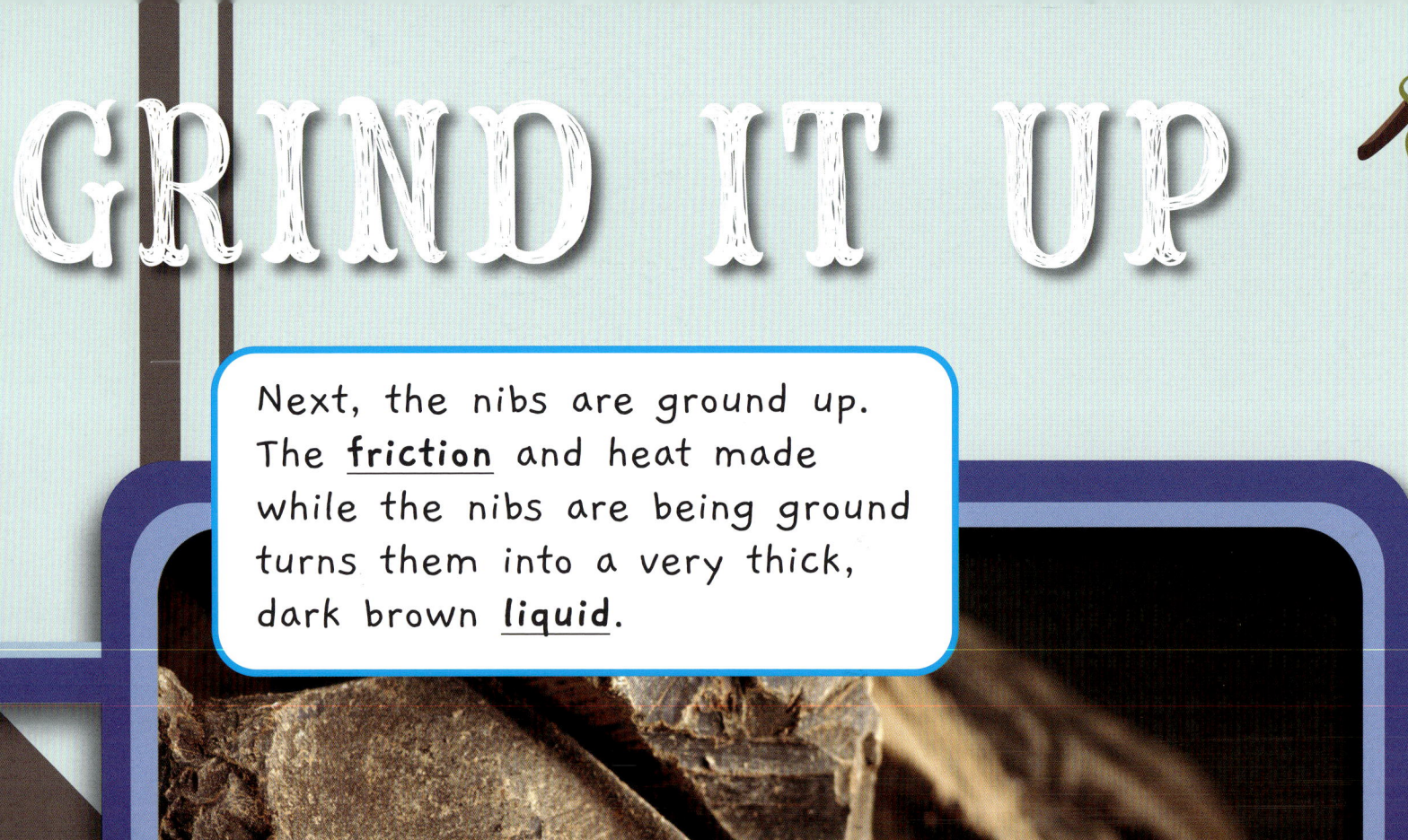

This is also known as cocoa mass.

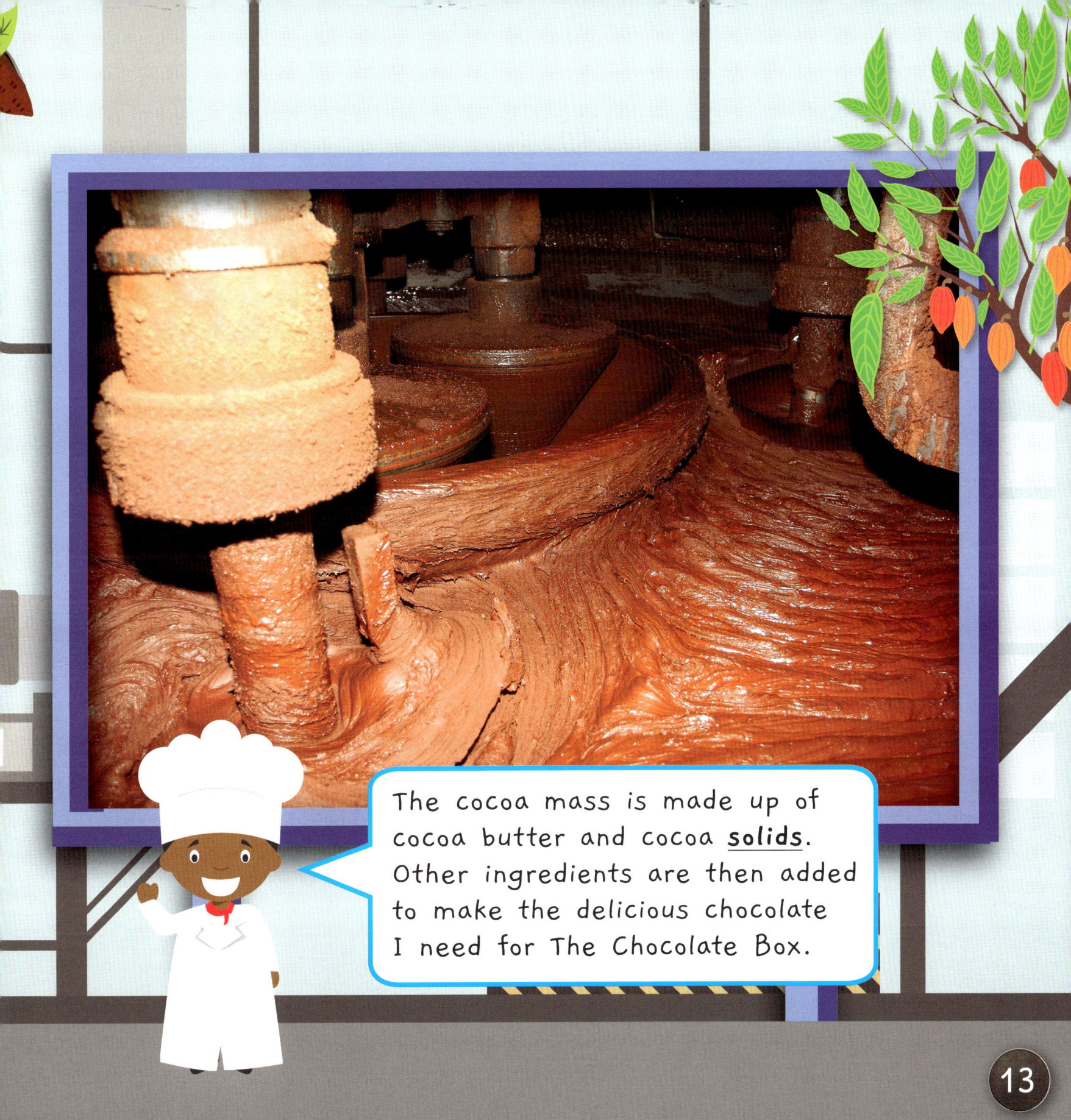

The cocoa mass is made up of cocoa butter and cocoa <u>solids</u>. Other ingredients are then added to make the delicious chocolate I need for The Chocolate Box.

# IN PRODUCTION

The mixture is then put into a machine called a conch. In the conch, the mixture is <u>kneaded</u> and rolled to become smooth.

This chocolate maker is cooling the chocolate down on a cool **surface**.

The mixture can be tempered. During tempering, the chocolate is heated and then cooled. This gives the chocolate a smooth and glossy shine.

My favourite shape is a star. What's yours?

The liquid chocolate is poured into moulds. These can be all different shapes such as bars, hearts, squares and stars.

After the mixture has been put into a mould, the mould is usually gently shaken to make sure there are no air bubbles and that the mixture perfectly fills its mould.

Once cooled, the bars are put into their packaging and sent to where they are being sold.

# SWEET CHOCOLATE

The sweet chocolate we enjoy is usually made from a mix of cocoa solids, cocoa butter and sugar. Each type of chocolate we enjoy has a different mix of these ingredients.

Milk chocolate is often made using cocoa solids, cocoa butter and has sugar and milk added to it.

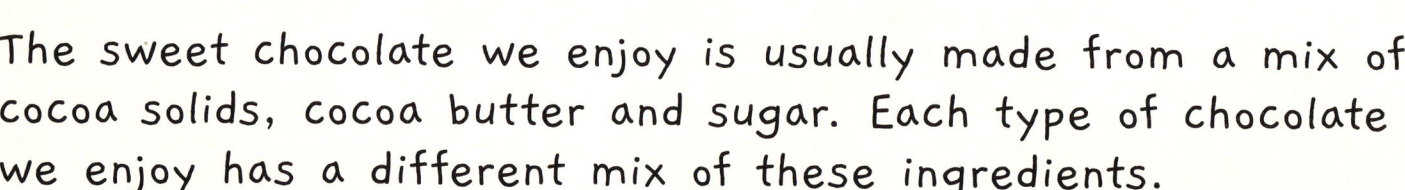

MILK CHOCOLATE

White chocolate usually has cocoa butter, sugar and milk but no cocoa solids.

WHITE CHOCOLATE

Dark chocolate often has cocoa solids, sugar and cocoa butter but no milk.

DARK CHOCOLATE

# ALL THE FLAVOURS

Some chocolate bars have a flavoured centre. This could be honeycomb, caramel, or **nougat**.

CARAMEL

HONEYCOMB

NOUGAT

Lots of different things can be added to chocolate. Nuts, fruit and fudge are all popular choices. What's your favourite type of chocolate?

Some people even enjoy eating chilli chocolate!

# CHOCOLATE TIME!

Phew! We've finished our journey and we've made it back with plenty of delicious chocolate. So, what can I get for you?

The Chocolate Box

**MENU**

Milk chocolate

Dark chocolate

White chocolate

Chocolate caramel

# GLOSSARY

| | |
|---|---|
| ferment | to go through a change over time |
| friction | the force created by rubbing one object against another |
| harvested | to have picked or gathered plants to be used by humans |
| kneaded | pressing, working and folding a mixture |
| liquid | a thing that flows, such as water |
| nougat | a type of sweet that usually contains nuts or pieces of fruit |
| pulp | the inner, juicy part of a fruit or vegetable |
| ripe | fully grown and ready to be picked |
| solids | things that hold their shape and are firm |
| surface | the top part of something |

# INDEX

beans 6–11
conches 14
fermentation 8–9
flavours 10, 20–21
Ghana 6
moulds 16–17
nibs 11–12
packaging 17
pods 7–8
pulp 8